Chef Teddy
Cooks Up Some Christmas Magic

Kusum Ravindranath's life changed when Teddy joined the family, with his big heart and bigger personality. When she's not outdoors with Teddy or a book, Kusum is a coach who helps her clients find joy through work, often against barriers. Her first book *Good Night and Good Luck* (Harper Collins India, 2011) was a heartfelt account of her roller coaster ride to finally getting a good night's sleep as a new mum. She lives in London with her husband, two daughters and Teddy. *Chef Teddy* is her first children's book.

For Lakshanaa who brought Teddy into our lives, And Shrikant who never let him leave.

Shashi Raghunandan is a proud dog dad with dreams of becoming a full-time dog walker, when he's not busy building his start-up from the ground up. A self-taught watercolour artist, Shashi has turned his love for painting into his very first adventure in illustrating *Chef Teddy*. He lives in the United States with his wife and their beloved toy poodle, Snoopy, who keeps their days delightfully furry and full of joy.

To my wonderful wife Joyita, and Snoopy, the best studio assistant a dog could be.

First published in 2025 by
Kusum Ravindranath, in partnership with
Whitefox Publishing Limited

www.wearewhitefox.com

Copyright © Kusum Ravindranath, 2025

EU GPSR Authorised Representative
LOGOS EUROPE, 9 rue Nicolas Poussin, 17000,
LA ROCHELLE, France
E-mail: Contact@logoseurope.eu

ISBN 978-1-9175237-3-8

Also available as an eBook
ISBN 978-1-9175237-4-5

Kusum Ravindranath asserts the moral right to be identified as the author of this work.

All rights reserved. No part of this publication may be reproduced, stored in a retrieval system or transmitted in any form or by any means, electronic, mechanical, photocopying, recording or otherwise, without prior written permission of the author.

Illustrated by Shashi Raghunandan
Project management by Whitefox Publishing Limited

Chef Teddy
Cooks Up Some Christmas Magic

Kusum Ravindranath ★ Shashi Raghunandan

This cold Christmas Eve
there's ice in the air,
and twinkling bulbs
shining light everywhere.

We're throwing a party for old friends and new. Sister and I are waiting, and Teddy's with us, too.

Mum and Dad will be cooking; they have big menu plans. They'll make delicious dishes; we'll be their helping hands.

Mum will roast the squash, with cranberry sequinned rice. There will be Yorkshire pudding and gravy with allspice,

and brussel sprout pakoras,
roast potatoes and peas,
glazed carrots, sticky chicken skewers
and creamy cauliflower cheese.

Dad will make the desserts:
A cream-filled chocolate yule,
plum cake, and iced mince pies.
We must try not to drool!

It's time to start the oven.
It's time to chop and grate.
But chef and sous chef are missing;
their train is running late.

So, who will roast the butternut squash?
And who will make the rice?
Who will fry the brussel sprouts?
And who will bake our pies?

Sister and I could bake a cake.
we could arrange the flowers.
But who will do the cooking?
They could be stuck for hours!

And then, suddenly we hear it...

...the sizzle of warm oil,
the clanging of saucepans,
the crackle of peppercorns,
the opening of cans.

It's TEDDY in our kitchen!
Wearing a toque and apron,
he's dicing at the table,
and juicing up a lemon.

'Teddy, what are you doing?'
in surprise, we scream.
'Do fetch the cauliflower,
for I'm the chef,' he beams.

We do what Teddy bids us,
as he works the garlic press.
He cooks a delicious curry,
but of course, he makes a mess.

There's chocolate on the ceiling.
There are carrots on the floor.
He bakes a perfect plum cake,
but there's custard on the door.

While Teddy chops and chiffons,
and starts to toss and stir,
we hoover the room and wipe it clean,
brush flour off Teddy's fur.

And just then...

Mum and Dad walk in,
faces streaked with worry.
Everyone likes to throw a party,
but not in such a hurry!

They smell the aroma of rosemary
on potatoes so buttery,
and see the feast on the table
laid out with shining cutlery.

They stand there, amazed.
They cannot believe their eyes,
and look at each other,
faces lit with surprise.

Crackers snap and glasses tinkle.
More friends are at the door.
Sister and I quietly watch
our little friend on the floor.

It's then we see the speck of herbs
still sitting on Teddy's nose.
Mum gives us a long, long look.
She'd wondered, now she knows.

Hours later...

The last guests leave; the plates are cleared.
Sister and I chant together,
'Here's to Teddy, super-chef,
 and our best friend forever!'

For Teddy has spent his whole life watching from the kitchen floor, as Mum and Dad sauté and stir, blend and bake, and more.

We whisper to him, 'Thank you, Teddy!
What a clever dog you are!'
Not just a sniffer, a crumb stealer or a licker...

Christmas Plum Cake Recipe

Ingredients

250g Dry fruits (mix of cranberries, dates, apricots, raisins)
120ml Orange juice
125g Unsalted butter
100g Brown sugar
100g Plain flour
50g Ground almond
1/2 tsp Baking powder
1 tsp Cinnamon powder and/or mixed spice
1 tsp Vanilla extract
2 Eggs

1. Preheat oven to 170°C

2. Chop the dry fruits. Put the chopped dry fruits in a saucepan, add the juice, butter and sugar, and place over medium heat until it boils.

3. Then simmer for 5 minutes. Let it cool.

4. Mix dry ingredients. In a bowl, whisk together the flour, ground almonds, baking powder, cinnamon and mixed spice.

5. Mix wet ingredients in another bowl – beat the eggs and vanilla.

6. Combine everything. Mix the flour into the fruit mixture. Then add the beaten eggs. Mix well.

7. Grease a cake tin, and pour in the batter. Bake at 170°C for about 45 minutes.

8. Cool and then decorate with icing sugar sprinkles or frosting.

www.ingramcontent.com/pod-product-compliance
Lightning Source LLC
Chambersburg PA
CBHW061152070526
44584CB00034B/4492